The Grief Bubble
helping kids explore and understand grief

by Kerry DeBay

and made very special and unique

by _____
(your name)

the Grief Bubble
helping kids explore and understand grief

copyright © 2007 by Kerry DeBay

Published June 2007 by Limitless Press LLC
http://www.limitlesspress.com ~ publisher@limitlesspress.com

Published simultaneously in paperback and eBook formats.

Paperback ISBN 10 digit: 0-9788681-4-5
Paperback ISBN 13 digit: 978-0-9788681-4-7

eBook ISBN 10 digit: 0-9788681-5-3
eBook ISBN 13 digit: 978-0-9788681-5-4

Library of Congress Control #: 2007928418

This book is designed to provide information in regard to the subject matter covered. It is sold with the understanding that the author/publisher is not engaged in rendering psychological services. If expert assistance or counseling is needed, the services of a competent professional should be sought.

This book is dedicated to
all of the healing hearts
who taught me about
grief through their
courage to feel
and to share.

thank you . . .

To the kids. . .

I am really glad that you have this book!
I made it especially for kids like you —
kids who have had something very
terrible happen in their lives, kids
who have had the "worst" happen,
like someone you love dying.

When the "worst" happens, lots of
things change. And change (little or
BIG) can bring on new, different,
or bigger feelings, thoughts, questions,
behaviors and sensations. It can
be confusing or painful or just really
really hard.

This book is just for you. It can help
you understand what is happening
in your head, your body, and your
heart.

And hopefully, it will help you feel better. It is a safe and special place for you to put your thoughts and feelings.

Maybe you can read this book with a grown-up — or maybe when you've finished it, you can share it with a grown-up. Sharing thoughts and feelings is one way to get them out... and getting them out can help you feel better.

I'm proud of you for using this book — grief can be a very hard thing to feel and to share and it takes a lot of courage to do hard things.

this book is just for you ♡

To the parents and other special adults caring for a grieving child...

○ Any change is a loss and can bring feelings of grief. The death of someone special is most likely the biggest change - the biggest loss - your child has experienced.

Grief at this scale may be a brand new experience. And even if it isn't, it can still be overwhelming and confusing.

It is important for children to understand that what they are experiencing is normal and that grief is a normal, natural response to loss. Remember that at different ages, children will understand and express their grief in different ways.

As a caring and supportive adult, it is important to:

♡ **Listen**... allow them to share their thoughts and stories without judgment.

♡ **Allow them to have their feelings**... ALL feelings - don't try to talk them out of feeling sad or angry or guilty. Let them know you hear what they've saying and that all feelings are okay to have.

♡ **Help them find safe ways to express their feelings**... while reinforcing that all feelings are natural and okay to have, assist them in recognizing, learning, and practicing safe ways to let the feelings out (like drawing, writing, talking to a trusted friend or adult, ripping up paper, running or exercising, making music...the list is as endless as your imaginations!)

♡ **Be a role model**... be aware of your relationship to the loss (or past losses). As you share your feelings and grief in a safe way, they will learn from you that it is normal and okay to have these feelings and there are safe & effective ways to cope with them.

How to use this book...

This book is intended to help children, ages 6 and older, to understand what grief is and to recognize their own grief. The interactive format invites them to find expression for their thoughts and feelings, encouraging an exploration of their grief.

The focus of the expression should not be on "quality" – there is no wrong or bad way to draw. This can be reinforced by not making judgments or suggestions as the child is creating, however encouraging them to draw whatever feels right to them.

If you find a child is "stuck" and asks you what to draw, responding with questions to help them figure it out will encourage their authentic expression...

... (e.g. what color do you think it should be? Is it big or small? What shape do you think it would have? Would it be a person or an animal or a thing?...)

○ Give permission for the images to <u>not</u> look like anything (use of abstract shapes) or to be symbols or even words. Invite the child to tell you about their images — and resist the temptation to tell them what you think it is before they tell you what they <u>know</u> it is! ○

And of course, provide encouragement and praise for doing this grief-work... because it <u>is</u> work and it can be hard.

your support is important and makes ♡ a difference!

What is grief?

have you ever heard that word before?

Once Upon a Time, life was normal.

normal life

(before someone special died)

what did your normal
life look like?

my normal life

draw a picture of your life before someone special died...

Sometimes the worst happens and everything changes...

someone
special
dies

↑ normal
life

what worst thing
happened in your life?

the worst thing

draw a picture of what happened...

and normal life....

...is...

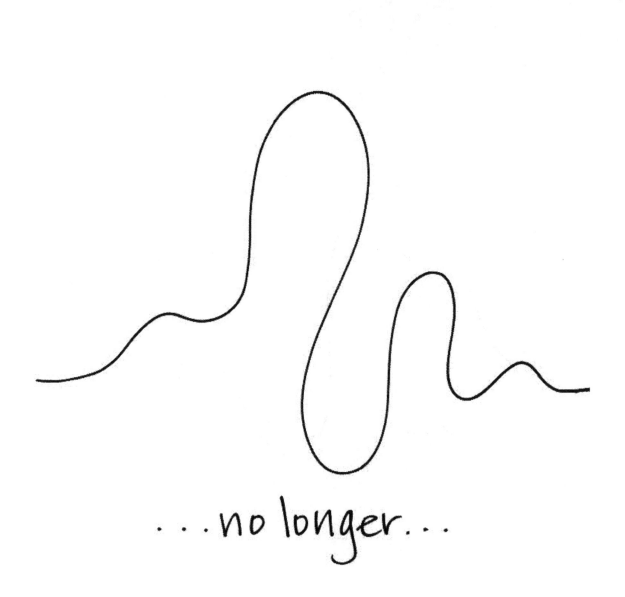

...no longer...

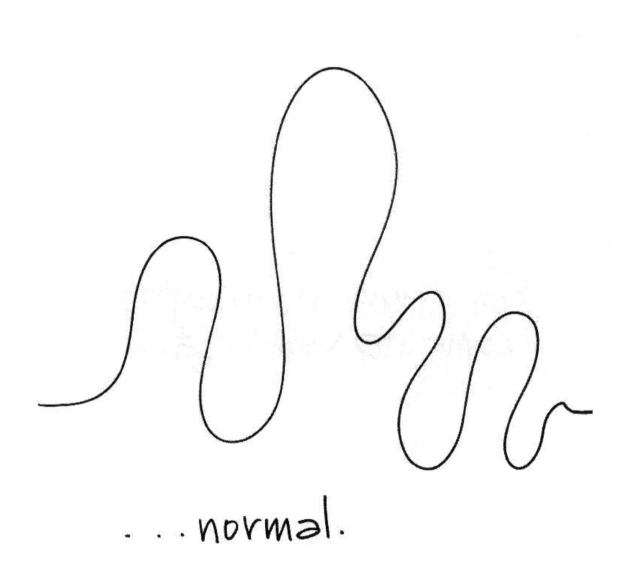

. . . normal.

sometimes new thoughts
come into your head...

...or you might have questions or memories...

What do you think about?

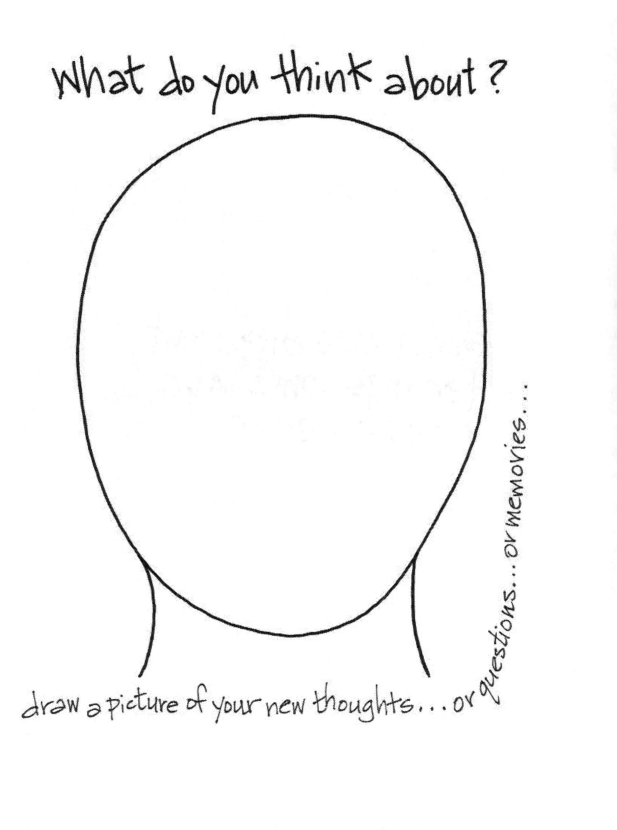

draw a picture of your new thoughts....or questions... or memories...

sometimes different
feelings come into
your heart....

...how many feelings can you name?

what feelings do you feel?

draw a picture of your feelings...

sometimes aches and pains
come into your body!...

...those are types of physical sensations...

what does your body feel like?

draw a picture of what's happening in your body...

sometimes you act
differently or do new things...

what are you doing differently?

draw a picture of what you do that's new or different...

all of these changes in your head, heart, and body are called **grief**. . .

such a little word for such big stuff!

what does your grief look like?

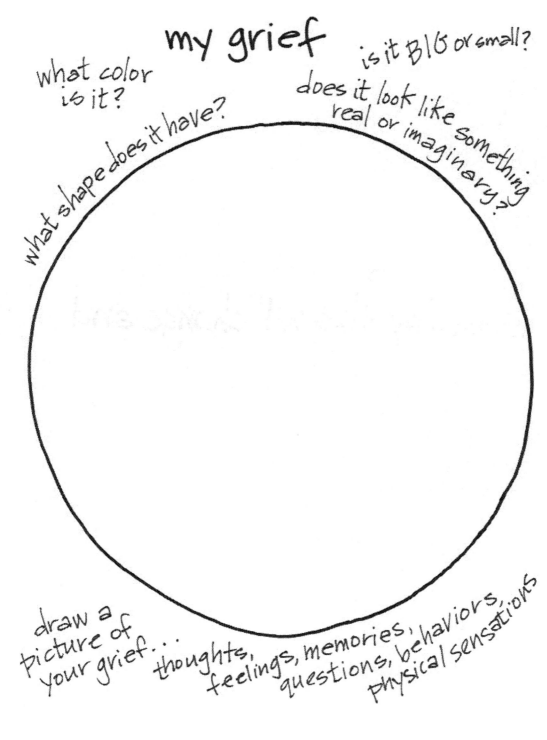

my grief

what color is it?

is it BIG or small?

does it look like something real or imaginary?

what shape does it have?

draw a picture of your grief...

thoughts, feelings, memories, questions, behaviors, physical sensations someday, this will change and

a new normal will happen....

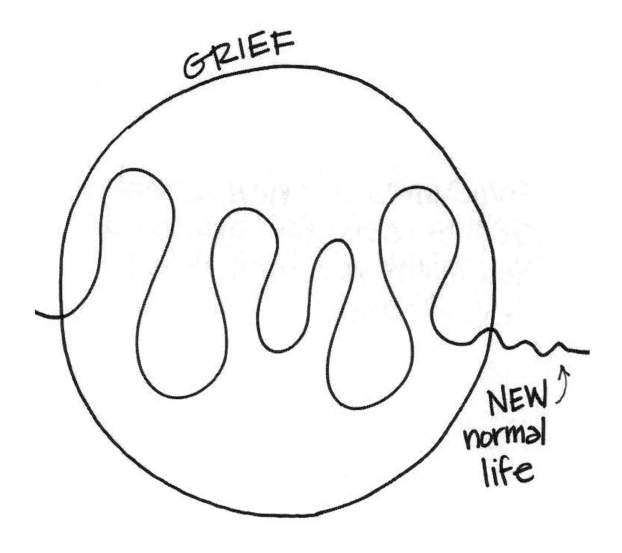

sometimes the new normal
seems really far away and
you might wonder if it will
ever come . . .

sometimes while you're
waiting for your new normal
life to happen, everything
can feel okay, even if just
for a little while. . . .

a few days. . . or longer!

a little while can be a few minutes. . . a few hours. . . a few

can you remember something
you were doing or someone
you were with during a
time that everything felt
okay (or better)?

a time when everything felt okay
(or at least a little bit better)

who are you with? what are you doing? where are you?

usually things will start to feel okay or better for longer times and more often...

...and you get closer and closer to your new normal life...

what would you like your
new normal life to look like?

my new normal life

where are you? what are you doing? who are you with? how do you feel!?

it's important to know that you've not alone - a lot of other kids have had the worst thing happen in their lives and have experienced grief, too. . .

some of these kids wanted
to share with you about
their grief and what helps...

let's see what they have to say! →

what is grief?

"Grief is your feelings when one of your loved ones die."
— Ashleigh, age 9

"Grief is an emotion that is sad and sometimes hard to control."
— Molly, age 7

"Grief means that my daddy died. It means that he lives in my heart. Your loved ones that died you can see in your heart. Because they are inside you."
— Lianna, age 4

"Well it doesn't matter who you lose but the shock kicks in and you don't want to do anything. Then you start to feel it. Like missing and stuff, that's what I think grief is."
— Kate, age 11

what do you think?

Grief is _____

_____

(your name)   (your age)

What helps?

"Talking about it, doing a hobby."
— Frankie, age 12

"Writing, speaking it to the air, but mostly speaking it to a loved one." — Alexandria, age 8

"Talk about it to a friend." — Seth, age 10

"What helps me with grief is hanging out with people my age that have gone through the same thing." — Alison, age 14

What helps you? (can you think of 5 things?)

1. _____   4. _____

2. _____   5. _____

3. _____

_____ _____
(your name)   (your age)

Thank you for using this book. I hope it helped.

Here are some more places to find help and to learn about grief:

For Kids...

"Badger's Parting Gifts", by Susan Varley

"Glad Monster Sad Monster," by Ed Emberley & Anne Miranda

"Molly's Mom died." by Margaret M. Holmes

"Sam's Dad died." by Margaret M. Holmes

"Someone I love died by suicide." by Doreen Cammarata

"When Dinosaurs Die." by Laurie Krasny Brown & Marc Brown

"When Someone Very Special dies," by Marge Heegaard

For adults...

"The Grieving Child." by Helen Fitzgerald

To find support in your area...

www.dougy.org
HospiceLink: 1-800-331-1620

About the author...

Kerry DeBay is a Board-Certified, Registered Art Therapist, Licensed Mental Health Counselor and a Certified Trauma Specialist. Kerry has been working with children and their families for over 15 years — a significant focus has been supporting children and their caregivers faced with the terminal illness or death of a loved one. The concept of the Grief Bubble came from this work with grieving children. The bubble developed as a way to illustrate and explain the phenomenon - grief - the children were experiencing, helping to increase their understanding and awareness of their unique process, while normalizing their experience.

Kerry currently resides in her beloved hometown of West Palm Beach, Florida where she passionately enjoys teaching and practicing yoga, running, and spending time with her family.

With sincere gratitude, I acknowledge those I have been blessed to encounter on my journey which led to this book:

♡ All of the children who inspired the Grief Bubble...

♡ Dharma and Vasanti, whose enthusiasm and efforts brought the book from dream to reality...

♡ the children of Hearts and Hope, Inc. who shared their thoughts on grief and coping and their families who supported this important contribution...

♡ My colleagues, who have played a significant part in my professional development and helped to refine and polish this book...

♡ Jashoda, who I admire for her ability to survive and thrive and the grace in her being — Ali and Frankie, who also contributed to this book and are always so present in their feelings and experiences...

♡ My family, whose support is priceless and who bring tremendous joy to my life...

. . . and a very special thank you to David for teaching me and Zoë for reminding me how profoundly a heart can be touched and changed by love and loss. ♡

To order additional copies
or to see the full catalog of
Limitless Press books, please visit
our website: www.limitlesspress.com

♡

Quantity discounts available.
Special pricing for Non-Profit
and educational organizations.
Contact publisher for more
information:
publisher@limitlesspress.com

contact Kerry! visit www.thegriefbubble.com